GRANDAD'S FUNERAL

KATE SKYLARK AND EMILY
WILKINS

Grandad's Funeral

A Heartbreaking True Story of Child Abuse,
Betrayal and Revenge

Disclaimer

This book is based on true events.

The names of people and places have been changed to protect the innocent.

Cover photograph is posed by a model and is used for illustrative purposes only

For every book sold, a donation will be made to the NSPCC

Contents

Chapter 1

I'm going to do it. I'm going to tell them all. I'm going to stand here, at my grandad's funeral and tell everyone the truth.

The church is full of people. I walk from my seat at the front of the church to the lectern. I am shaking from head to foot. I have a piece of paper in my hand with a speech, telling a story of a kindly grandfather, a man I respected and looked up to, a man who taught me maths, read me Dickens and told me about politics. But I'm not going to read that. No, I'm finally going to tell the truth.

Because you see, I have a Secret. It's a Secret I've been carrying with me for years. A Secret that has messed with my head for long enough. It's caused me to feel unspeakable shame, given me panic attacks and nightmares, and has led to my suffering with a serious eating disorder. My physical health, my mental health and my relationship with my family have all suffered because of this Secret. And it's time the Secret was told.

I'm going to tell them all that Len Wilkins, my grandfather, was not the wonderful, clever exceptional man they all think he is. He was not a 'pillar of society'. He was not a great, or even a respectable man. I'm going to tell them that he sexually abused me in the vilest way when I was only eleven years old. I'm going to tell them what he really was. He was evil, and I'm going to tell them all.

I climb the stairs of the lectern. Four steps. Only four. I actually count them as I go up and wish there were more. At the top I stop and look at the faces of the congregation.

Finally, I'm going to tell them all…

…and I open my mouth to speak.

Chapter 2

It all began when my baby brother, Marcus, was born. I remember distinctly the night that Mum was rushed to hospital, in an ambulance, blood pouring down her legs. It was the most terrifying night of my eleven-year-old life. The sight I remember the most was of Mum being helped into the back of the ambulance, still in her nightie. Her big pregnant tummy was sticking out, making the nightie stretch tight, and her belly button was poking out through the thin material. The bottom of the pink nightie was drenched red with blood. It was like something out of a horror film.

The baby wasn't due yet, I knew that. And although Dad told me not to worry, even at that age

I realised something was very wrong, that something very serious was happening.

My sister, Pauline, and I sat up almost all night, waiting for news. We watched television until late, trying not to think of the horror we had just seen, trying not to think the awful thought that was going through both our heads. Was Mum going to be okay? It's a terrible thought for any child, to imagine their mother dying. Eventually, I know I fell asleep because the next thing I remember was the phone ringing and Pauline answering it because she was the older sister.

I don't know exactly what Dad said to her but I could tell it was good news. Pauline just kept saying, 'Thank God! Oh, thank God!'

'Emily, Mum's okay and the baby's out,' Pauline said as soon as she put the phone down. 'It's a little boy. We've got a brother!' I remember starting to cry, without knowing why.

No one told me at the time, but apparently my mum needed four pints of blood to save her life. She had had a severe placental abruption and that had caused the bleeding. The doctors told her not to try to get pregnant again. My little brother was born by emergency caesarean section, two months premature. Tiny baby Marcus went straight into an incubator in the special care baby unit to help his little lungs to breathe. He only weighed three and a half pounds.

When Mum was better and came home from hospital, she didn't bring the new baby. He was too small and weak to leave special care. It must have been a tough and terrible time for Mum and Dad in the weeks after Marcus was born. The baby was going to have to live in the incubator for many weeks or even months. The doctors told Mum and Dad it would be some time before he would be strong enough to be able to breathe on his own and come home. I suppose there must have been a danger that he would never come home at all. But that fact was never mentioned to us girls.

Pauline and I only went in to the hospital to see him a couple of times while he was there. We could look through the see-through sides of the incubator. He looked like a scrunched up caterpillar with his little knees folded up under him, and his skin looked a bit like a newborn baby bird, all red and wrinkly. But we couldn't hold him or even touch him, in case we made him ill. His immune system was so weak there was a big risk of infection. Even a little bit of dirt or a normal common cold would have made Marcus terribly ill and might even have killed him. Only Mum and the nursery nurses were allowed to touch Marcus, and only after sterilising their hands over and over. So we didn't hold or touch or play with our baby brother for a long time. He couldn't even have a teddy bear in the incubator to keep him company.

As you probably know, it's not good for newborn babies to be separated from their mums because they need to bond with their mothers from the moment they are born. This meant Mum almost had to live in the hospital with baby Marcus. I suppose it must have been really difficult. But if you think about it, she was still weak herself from the operation and from the traumatic birth, so maybe hospital was the best place for her.

Dad went to see the baby in hospital almost every day too. Sometimes we had a babysitter or went to a friend's house after school. But most of the time it was down to my thirteen-year-old sister, Pauline, to look after eleven-year-old me, all by herself and for long periods of time.

Mum and Dad didn't think this was fair on either of us. Pauline had often babysat me in the evening for a few hours if Mum and Dad had gone out. But the end of term was just a couple of weeks away. During the summer holiday we girls would be home all day, and it was too much to expect Pauline to become my full-time childminder.

Mum and Dad made the decision to take me out of school early and send me to live with my nanna and grandad. They clearly thought this was a fine plan. I would go to Wales to live with Nanna and Grandad while Mum and Marcus recovered. I would live there until the end of the summer holiday, or until Marcus could come home if that was sooner. Pauline, who was that bit older, would be fine to stay home. She was to spend some of the time alone at home. But she would also be able to go to stay at her best friend Deborah's house whenever she wanted.

'It will be such fun for you, Emily,' said Dad. 'You can go to the beach every day with Nanna. And Grandad can do some lessons with you so you don't miss any schoolwork.'

Grandad had been a teacher until he retired a few years ago, so it all made sense, according to Dad.

Chapter 3

I remember not being too happy about the plan to stay with my grandparents. For a start, I would miss Sports Day at school. Sports Day was one of my favourite days of the whole of the school year. I was an athletic child and I would normally win several 'medals'. (The medals were just different coloured badges that we pinned to our school jumpers but they meant the world to us.) Besides this, I really wasn't looking forward to a whole summer away from Pauline and all my friends.

But there was an even bigger reason that I wasn't looking forward to the stay in Wales. I liked my nanna, but I was petrified of my grandad.

Grandad was probably not yet sixty at the

time, but to me he seemed ancient, like an old, old man. He was a stern and angry man who had little time or inclination to play with us. He was very serious and I almost never saw him laugh. Granddad was the absolute head of the family and everyone looked up to him. You could tell that Dad really loved him and always tried desperately to please him, but Mum sometimes called him 'a tyrant'.

As a young man, Granddad had gone to university when it was still very unusual for a working class man to do so. He spent most of his life as a maths teacher at the local boys' grammar school.

Granddad had taken early retirement from the grammar school some years before. On leaving the school, he paid for a trophy to be named for him – 'The Len Wilkins Maths Cup', which was to be awarded each year to the pupil who most excelled in mathematics. I never saw the cup, but apparently it was a huge trophy that dwarfed all the other trophies in the cabinet.

The official story of Granddad's retirement was that he had to stop work when he developed heart problems. But my mother used to tell a different story. She said that when the school stopped being a grammar school and became a normal comprehensive, Granddad just couldn't cope with the riffraff and low-intelligence of the working class boys he was suddenly expected to teach. He was a terrible intellectual snob and would frequently ridicule people for not understanding something. Suddenly faced, not with the middle-class and well-behaved boys the 11 plus had creamed off, but with a perfectly normal bunch of 'ordinary' children, my granddad couldn't cope. Mum said he eventually had a nervous breakdown and was pensioned off. It really doesn't say much for his teaching ability or his attitude to children.

Granddad was so proud, and so pompous and he always seemed critical of our school performance, no matter how well we did. We girls were both quite academic, especially Pauline. But it was never good enough for Granddad. On the few times that Pauline or I did impress him with our intelligence, or with our progress at school, Granddad would only use it as a reason to boast that he was the one responsible for that – it was his genes, his bloodline that had been the reason for our success. It was never a congratulation for us, when we did well, but for him. Honestly, from the way he spoke, it was as if *he* had been the one who had got an A for an essay!

The funny thing was that he was a terrible teacher! I remember him trying to teach me algebra at the age of about eight or nine and getting really frustrated that I didn't understand. I remember looking at the sum he had put in front of me and trying so hard to work it out. I was so afraid of him and so wanted to impress him, to make him like me. I took the pencil and with some pride, 'solved' the algebra puzzle he had put in front of me. But I had mistaken the little x symbol for the normal x of a times table problem and so the answer I had come up with was hopelessly wrong. No wonder I couldn't solve it, I was eight years old! But Granddad was furious.

'What do they teach in school these days?' he said. 'I won prizes for algebra and so did your dad. So you can't have got this from our side of the family!'

Some teacher he was!

I did like my Nanna and she was very kind to us when we were little children. Nanna was also very proud. She was a terrible snob, but of a different kind to Granddad. I always thought she was a bit like that Hyacinth Bouquet lady from the

TV series. She was always talking about people who were 'common', and calling people 'gypsies' just because they weren't dressed as smartly as she was. She would boast continually about the silliest little thing, comparing herself constantly with others and finding faults in everyone else around her. She would talk incessantly to no one in particular saying things like, 'Everyone always says I've got the cleanest washing in the street. Mrs Thomas asked me yesterday, how *do* you get those shirts so white?'

'Of course, she only serves pink salmon, but in this house, I only ever have red.'

'Let me show you the birthday card she sent, it's like a postage stamp compared to the one I sent her.'

That sort of nonsense came out of her mouth every day. Nanna was also terrified of foreigners, especially black people, who she always called 'blackies'. Every Asian or Arab or brown-skinned person she called a 'Pakistani'. The funny thing is, I don't know if she had ever met a black or Asian person in her life. There were none living in her town when we were children so she certainly didn't meet any in her day-to-day life. But that didn't stop her blaming every reported burglary or crime on Pakistanis, blackies or gypsies.

Nanna's favourite boast was to talk of Grandad as a 'very great man'. I've asked my mum about this in later years. Apparently, Grandad had been a 'bit of a catch'. He was the only man from the village who had gone to university, and had been very handsome when he was young. Nanna came from a very poor background, even for rural Wales, so she must have been thrilled to bag herself a husband she probably thought was out of her league. But she boasted so much about her husband's intelligence and importance that sometimes when I think about it now, I wonder if she was trying to convince herself it was true. Although back then, I listened to the tales of my amazingly talented and brilliant grandfather, and I believed every word.

Chapter 4

I know I was always excited to go to visit my grandparents, and I did enjoy our twice yearly trips to the west coast of Wales, where Nanna and Grandad lived. But mainly I liked it because I enjoyed the long drive in the car with the family. We would sing songs and stop at the new Gordano motorway service station near the Clifton Suspension Bridge. This seemed like the most exciting place in the whole world, so glamorous and exotic with all its computer games and modern space-age cafe. It would look hopelessly dated now, but back then it seemed like Disneyland.

And so it was in early July, a fortnight away from the end of school term, that I was plucked from school, told to say goodbye to my sister and Mum and driven by my dad to Wales. As a treat, Dad stopped as usual at the Gordano services and bought me fish and chips. He also bought a whole pile of comics, almost all the ones we could see. There were girls' comics like Jinty and Misty, and funny ones like the Beano and the Beezer. He also got some puzzle magazines for me, word-searches and children's crosswords, something I really liked. I would normally only ever get one comic a week, so this was an unusual treat. I think perhaps Dad was feeling a little sorry for me. Or perhaps he just felt a bit sad that I was going away for so long.

I want to say from the outset, that my mum and dad were great parents. They loved all of us children and were always there for us. What happened to me wasn't their fault at all and I don't blame them for a thing. Dad idolised Grandad and I know that if he had any idea what was going to happen to me at the hands of Grandad, he would never have left me with him.

It's funny the things you remember as a child. Pulling up outside the grey stone-clad terraced house. The plastic red roses in a vase in the window, in front of a big net curtain. The glass panel above the door with the name of the house in Welsh. The ding-dong doorbell. The waddling shape of my nanna appearing in the misty glass of the front door. Her high-pitched squealing Welsh accent as she greeted us. The feeling of oppressive heat the moment we walked in.

Their house was always too hot. And it also had a sort of muffled feel about it. There were too many cushions and ticking clocks and it always felt claustrophobic, like being wrapped in hot blankets. They had lots of china plates hanging on the walls and horse brasses on the fireplace. There were pictures of cute crying children holding puppies and dozens of frames on the china cabinet containing photos of me, my sister and cousins. Taking pride of place above the fireplace was a hideous painting of a windmill scene which I always hated, even as a little child.

Nanna was very proud of her cooking and forced food onto us constantly as a matter of pride. If she wasn't making a meal, she was making tea and cakes. If no one wanted tea, she'd bring out the sweets and chocolate. All the food that Nanna made was overcooked. The vegetables were all like mush and had lost their colour. She made gravy that looked like tar. When she cooked steak, she didn't grill or fry it. Instead, she would roast it to death in the oven covered in a pan lid so that it was like eating leather. Nothing ever really tasted of anything.

Nanna and Grandad ate the same thing on the same day of every week. Every Friday they had fish cooked in the oven with chips. On Sunday they would have a roast chicken with mushy veg. Another day was tinned salmon with potatoes and salad, and one day was reserved for sausage and mash with thick brown gravy. One day for the leathery steak. Pudding was always the same: tinned fruit salad, pears or peaches in heavy syrup with evaporated milk poured over the top.

The one saving grace in Nanna's cooking was the cakes. She baked constantly, eating cake at least three times a day. My favourite was little sponge cakes spread with jam and dipped in desiccated coconut. Others in her repertoire included shortbread and sultana-studded rock cakes. These were always served sitting at the flowery three-piece suite.

Tea was served several times a day, whether you wanted it or not, and it always came in a tinkly bone china cup and saucer with a silver spoon. Balancing cake on a plate and cup and saucer was never easy. Whenever I hear that tinkling of a bone china cup and saucer, my heart sinks as my mind goes back to Nanna and Grandad's house, sitting on the sofa, trying not to spill crumbs on the carpet or tea on my knee.

Grandad didn't ever lift one single finger to help Nanna. Even though he didn't work anymore, he never even did any of the usual man's jobs like washing up or taking the bins out. He wouldn't go to get his dinner from the kitchen or take his plate in when he was finished. He would just sit and wait for Nanna to bring his plate in, and then wait while she took it away. She would even sprinkle salt on his dinner for him and put sugar in his tea while he sat and watched her. Once Nanna came to visit us, leaving Grandad on his own. Apparently, he lived on nothing but jam sandwiches for the entire weekend. By the time she got home, he was furious and sitting cross-armed and tight-lipped, waiting for her to cook him some proper food.

I know this is true because it was Nanna who told me. But rather than be angry or ashamed of his behaviour, she almost seemed proud of how useless he was. It was as if his inability to even feed himself just showed up what a wonderful wife she really was the rest of the time. He just couldn't do without her. She used to joke, 'If I go first, he'll starve to death'. And she said this with some pride.

They never drank alcohol, Nanna and Grandad. Mum used to joke that if Grandad would only have a beer occasionally it might melt the stick up his arse.

Grandad liked to sit in a chair, smoke cigarettes, and shout at the television. He was a big supporter of the Labour party and had a lot of respect for James Callaghan. But Mum tells me it was only because the alternative at the time was Margaret Thatcher and Grandad would never support a woman leader.

Dad also had two much older sisters, my aunties Sheila and Valerie. I liked my aunties a lot but I know they didn't get on with Nanna and Grandad and I can't remember us ever all getting together as a family. It was only many years later that I would go on to discover why that was.

I remember Dad giving me a hug before he left. I ran to the front window to wave him goodbye as he drove off, pulling the curtain to one side. The curtain was embroidered in white net with a huge ploughing scene – a shire horse pulling an old-fashioned plough behind. I loved that curtain as a child and thought it was beautiful. I hated it as an adult.

Chapter 5

It wasn't so bad at first at Nanna's. She took me to the seaside and bought me ice cream, waddling along the seafront in her little heels. Nanna was very fat but she always dressed nicely and wore court shoes with heels. She always wore a hat as if she was going to a wedding, and often she'd wear white gloves. She would take me shopping too, and often to visit her friend, Mrs Evans. I thought it was funny the way she always used to call Mrs Evans 'Mrs Evans', even though she was a friend. Nanna never called her Sue or Mary or Barbara or whatever Mrs Evans's first name was. But I noticed that a lot of Welsh people used to do the same.

Whenever we went to visit Mrs Evans we'd eat cake and drink tea. I really liked Mrs Evans. She had a little Pekingese dog called Pushkin. He was really fluffy and liked to be brushed. I'd sit and brush him while the ladies talked. Mrs Evans would wink at me with a big smile, so I knew she was a kind person. In her dining room there was a big load of toys for when her grandchildren came to visit. The toys were a bit young for me because her grandchildren were only little at the time. But I still liked to play with them. I'd play with the toys or the dog while the ladies would drink tea and do nothing but gossip about the people they knew.

'He caught a chill in his tooth. It went to his brain, and he died.'

'She looked a state in that hat. Who did she think she was?'

'More gypsies moved in on the recreation ground.'

'He's young enough to be her son so shameful.'

I always assumed that Mrs Evans was Nanna's best friend because she would visit her several times every week. But Nanna didn't always act like a best friend. Whenever we left Mrs Evans's house and were walking down the road home, Nanna would say things like, 'Did you see the state of those tea stains on the china? Tea stains! Hasn't she ever heard of bleach in a teacup? And she's still wearing the shoes she bought for Grace Davis's wedding. I haven't seen her in a new pair of shoes in three years. And that dog all over the babies' things, unhygienic, that's what it is.'

When we'd get home Nanna would take off her pretty pointed shoes and put her feet in a washing up bowl full of water and Epsom salts. I was shocked to see that her feet looked horrible with gnarly red toes, all folded over each other and big callouses on the sides.

'What's wrong with your toes, Nanna?' I asked.

'My toes?' She said the word 'toes' like 'taws', like they do in that part of Wales. 'That's forty years and never a day in less than a two-inch heel, that's what that is!' she said proudly, showing off her ugly feet. Nanna's very favourite pastime was to boast about herself, about the things people were saying about her, or were thinking about her, or the way they were jealous of her.

'I could see her thinking, "How *does* that Gladys Wilkins dress so smartly on a teacher's pension?"'

'"That Gladys Wilkins," they say. "She wears better shoes than the Queen,"' says Nanna, talking about herself.

'I know why she came round, it was so she can brag to all the women at the club that she's calling on Gladys and Len Wilkins. *That* will have got them all talking. It's not everyone that gets an invitation to our house.'

I don't think for one moment those women were bragging about visiting Nanna's house. I don't think anyone probably ever noticed whether she was wearing a two-inch heel or flat shoes. I don't believe anyone ever thought her shoes were better than the Queen's. I don't think any of Nanna's fantasies were true at all. To be honest, I don't even know if she believed it herself. I think what's more likely is those thoughts would go through her head like daydreams, and then she would repeat them as if they had really happened.

She was always wittering on, boasting away as she made the tea and dusted things. I don't know if she was talking to Grandad because he never replied and hardly ever took any notice of the things she said. Sometimes, if she mentioned the gypsies or the blacks or someone shameful, Grandad would perk up and reply.

'I don't know why you've been talking to that Beryl Matthews anyway,' he would say, 'what with her husband on the bins.' ('On the bins' meant he worked as a bin man and therefore his wife wasn't fit company for our family.) But mostly, he just ignored her and carried on watching the television, reading the paper and smoking his cigarettes.

Another time Grandad would get involved in her conversations was when Nanna would talk about what a particular woman was wearing. He seemed to have a lot to say about women's clothes, particularly whether they were 'tarty' or 'shameful'. And the thing he got most angry about was young teenage girls dressed in revealing clothes. Sometimes the television news would have a report of a sexual assault that had happened somewhere in the country.

'And what was she wearing, walking out at two o'clock in the morning, that's what I'd like to know,' he would boom in his big pompous voice. 'No wonder these girls are all getting attacked these days. Is it surprising when they go out showing more flesh than the day they were born? They've only got themselves to blame.'

One day while I was staying there, I came down in the morning wearing my thin summer dress with little straps that showed my shoulders. He took one look at me and told me to 'go and put some clothes on!' I soon learned that I couldn't wear that dress without a cardigan, even when it was very hot, without Grandad disapproving. He also didn't like it when I wore shorts or anything that showed too much skin. It was a hot summer but I ended up wearing jeans for most of the time. It was easier that way.

On Sundays, Nanna and Grandad would go to church, always. Grandad was something important in the church, a warden or whatever, although I've never known what that means. Before that first Sunday, Nanna took me out to buy some new shoes. She told me I needed white shoes if I'm to come to church with her and Grandad. So she took me to the little shoe shop in town and bought me white strappy sandals which I absolutely loved.

'Is this your Gareth's girl?' the lady shop assistant asked Nanna.

'Yes, his youngest one. They've just had a boy but he's in the hospital and I'm to take care of the little one. Her mother's ailing too, after the birth.' And then Nanna added, 'She's not strong like our side of the family. I had my three all at home. And never made a moment's fuss. After Gareth, I was up doing the washing after two hours.'

Nanna also took me to buy a new coat, a white one with gold buttons. I absolutely loved that coat. It looked so nice against my long blonde hair.

That Sunday, Nanna dressed me in my new coat and new shoes ready for church. She brushed out my hair one hundred times and tied back the top of my hair with a ribbon.

'Now you'll get to sit up front with your Grandad and me,' she said as we entered the churchyard. 'But don't you dare turn your head as you walk up the aisle. They'll all be looking, but you keep your dignity and eyes front, young lady. They need to know what side of the family *you* take after.'

So the three of us walked up the aisle to the front seats of the church as if we were the royal family. Nanna and Grandad walked slower than everyone else, just to make sure everyone noticed them. I didn't look around once. And it did feel nice, walking up to the front of the church with everyone looking at us, and thinking we were special. I held my head up and felt proud in my new white sandals and my smart new coat. Nanna and Grandad were both good singers, and once upon a time they were in the church choir. Grandad sang the hymns in a deep booming voice and Nanna sang in a high-pitching trill, with lots of vibrato. They seemed to sing louder than everyone else in the church and I did wonder what everyone else was thinking of them, as they sat up the front, taking all the attention.

On one of our church visits, we arrived at the front seats to find a young family sitting in our usual place. Perhaps they were new to the church and didn't realise the front seats weren't for the likes of them. Grandad didn't even speak to them. He just sort of flicked his hand as if to swipe them away, like flies. And, unbelievably, without saying a single word, the family got up and moved to a different part of the church, even though there was plenty of room on that pew for all of us.

So that's the sort of people they were, my nanna and grandad. They were pompous and snobbish and stuck-up. They were small-minded and judgemental. But I have to say, until this point, they hadn't been cruel or nasty or even particularly strict with me. I was allowed to stay up quite late, I didn't have to do any odd jobs, and other than at mealtimes, they didn't make me follow many rules. Mum and Dad had always laughed about Nanna's constant boasting.

I think they saw her as a silly and harmless old lady, nothing more. And at that point, so did I.

For the first few nights I desperately missed Mum and Dad and Pauline. But I soon settled in and got used to my bedroom, to the heat of the house, and all the cake. I actually began to have quite a nice time in those first few weeks. I liked going with Nanna to visit her friends. I liked helping her bake. I liked going to the seaside all the time and I liked playing in the garden because we only lived in a flat at home.

I was still afraid of Grandad and I followed Nanna wherever she went. But at this point, Grandad hadn't really done anything wrong. He was just a scary old man, but there seemed to be no harm in him. He often watched children's television with me and never told me to change the channel. Sometimes he helped me fill in one of my crosswords. And when he shouted at a politician on the television, I would nod in agreement, hoping to get his approval. So for those first couple of weeks, things were actually going quite well.

It was after about a fortnight of being there that it all went wrong. Because that's when it all began. And it happened at night.

Chapter 6

There were three bedrooms upstairs at Nanna and Grandad's house. At one end of the landing was my dad's old room, at the other was Nanna and Grandad's room. I was to sleep in the middle room, the spare room, which used to be where my two aunties slept.

I remember every single tiny detail of that room. I know there were roses on the wallpaper and thick rose-covered curtains. I remember there was a chest of drawers covered in a lacy tablecloth. On the chest of drawers was one of those big jugs sitting in a basin that people used to use to wash in the olden days.

It was very old-fashioned even then, but I remember thinking how posh it made the room look.

There was also a chair in the corner of the room with a padded seat. When you lifted the seat of the chair, there was a potty under the seat to go to the toilet in. I always thought that was very funny. I mean, who would ever think of going to the toilet in their own bedroom?

The bed was a big, high double bed, and seemed like the biggest bed I had ever seen. It had big round bed-knobs on the four bed posts like the one in *Bedknobs and Broomsticks.* I loved it because I felt like the princess from *The Princess and the Pea* when I got up into that huge bed every night. Nanna always put nylon sheets on the bed, and a pink quilted nylon bedspread. I always thought the bedding felt horrible, slimy and plastic and hot. But even with the nylon sheets, I still loved that big bed. Those two weeks in the *Princess and the Pea* bed were probably the first time in my life when I actually looked forward to going to bed. But all that was going to change.

I woke up one night to find someone in my room. It was dark but I could see a human shape standing over me. But the person wasn't just standing there. They were fumbling about, doing something. I soon recognised who it was. It was just light enough in the room for me to tell it was Grandad. I began to wake up a little more, and I realised the covers of the bed had been taken right down past my feet and Grandad had his hand up inside my nightgown. He was fiddling with the elastic on my knickers.

'Grandad?' I murmured. 'What are you doing?'

Grandad just put his other hand to his mouth, put one finger up against his lips and said, *'Shhhhhttttt!'* He said it angrily, with a frown on his face, like he would if I have been naughty for making a noise. He continued to fiddle his way inside my knickers and fumble around with his fingers for some time. I was too afraid of him to answer back, so I just laid there while he groped me. Eventually he removed his hand and just left the room without ever saying a word.

I had no idea what had just happened. I didn't really understand it at all. But I don't think I was afraid or even particularly upset that first time and I think I fell asleep again quite quickly.

The next morning at breakfast, Grandad seemed perfectly normal. If anything, he was a little more cheerful than usual. He even seemed a bit more affectionate and offered to read me some Dickens. He always liked to say *David Copperfield* is the greatest book ever written. I didn't really enjoy Dickens at the age of eleven. I thought it was old-fashioned and boring and the people were always talking in silly ways. But I was so thrilled Grandad was actually showing an interest in me. So I readily agreed to be read to, in Grandad's booming monotonous voice. I even sat on his lap.

In my silly childish brain, I felt glad that he came to my bedroom that night. I don't think I actually knew what he was doing. It certainly didn't cross my mind that it was anything sexual. I do remember thinking that perhaps his fiddling about was his way of showing affection. Dad always told me it's hard for old men to show their feelings, they came from a different time when men were different. It was hard for Grandad to show he loved me, but for a short while, I really believed he did.

That first night was just the beginning. Because night after night, he kept coming to my room at night and fiddling around with me. I didn't like it but because it was Grandad I just let him do it. He was the boss of this family and I wouldn't dare to go against him.

Chapter 7

I started to warm a little to Grandad even though he was doing this to me almost every night. Bedtime had become really confusing and sometimes a bit scary, but at least he was being so much nicer to me during the day times.

But he was still such an angry, scary man. I remember being in the kitchen with Nanna and watching a football come sailing past the window into the garden. Clearly some child from a neighbouring house had kicked a little too hard.

'Nanna, shall I go and throw the ball back?' I offered. But Grandad had seen it too. He got up from his armchair, picked up a knife from the kitchen drawer and stormed out the back door. He went over to the football, picked it up and stabbed it with the knife, then threw it back in the direction it came. He came back into the house with a face like thunder, threw the knife in the sink and sat back in his chair.

'I've told them enough times now to keep their bloody balls in their own garden. I told them what would happen next time I saw a ball damaging my plants!'

Nanna and Grandad's garden was a scrubby wasteland of patchy grass surrounded by a crumbling grey breeze-block wall, and I never once saw either of them do any gardening. So I'm not even sure there were any plants there to damage.

Shortly afterwards, we heard the doorbell go. It was the dad of the boys whose football Grandad had punctured. He was standing at the door, looking a bit sheepish. It seemed everyone was a bit afraid of Grandad. The man was holding the half-flat football and standing next to his son, who was about seven years old and looked like he'd been crying.

'Len, really!' said the man. 'Was that really necessary? Did you need to do *this*?' he said, holding out the ball. 'That was one of Mark's birthday presents. He's got some boys over for a party and they got a bit excited with the football, that's all.'

'Don't you 'Len' me! I'll thank you to call me Mr Wilkins, you little ruffian!' Grandad shouted at the man as if he was a child himself. 'Just when did you get so big for your boots anyway, David Jones? Or should I say "Pisser"? That's what they called you, wasn't it? After you pissed yourself on the trip to Bridgend?'

Then I realised, this man was one of Grandad's old pupils. That was why he was speaking to him as if he was a child. Grandad then spoke to the little boy, Mark.

'Did you know your dad used to piss his pants at school so much, the other children called him Pisser? Stank, it did.'

David Jones just went quiet. He didn't look at his boy, who was staring up at him.

'I'll get you a new football and you can just play in the park from now on, lad,' he said quietly, still not looking at Mark.

Grandad slammed the door and then spent the next half hour shouting stories, to no one in particular, about David 'Pisser' Jones and his weak bladder. I couldn't believe what I had seen. I felt so sorry for Mark and for his dad. How could Grandad be so mean?

Can you imagine this happening today? It just wouldn't be possible. If there were a teacher today who was as mean as Grandad, he would be sacked. He would be disciplined and maybe even charged. Children like David Jones would get compensation for what they suffered. But back when Grandad was working as a teacher, cruel, harsh behaviour meant everyone assumed you were a really good teacher.

'He's very strict, very harsh, but a really good teacher,' my dad would say. I would say that if you're strict and harsh then that means you're *not* a good teacher!

Grandad did get a bit of a come-uppance for the football incident. Later that day he discovered all the tyres of his car had been let down. He was incandescent with rage as he called the police, telling them his tyres 'had been slashed'. I remember a local policeman coming to the door.

'So what's this then, Len?' asked the policeman. 'Crime of the century, is it?' he said in a jokey, friendly way.

And then Grandad stood in front of that policeman and told an absolute pack of lies! He said that the neighbour, David Jones, and a party of boys had been trespassing, playing football in his garden, and when Grandad tried to defend himself and his property, the gang then vandalised his car.

'We don't feel safe in our house,' said Grandad. 'They are a public nuisance, that family.'

But the policeman couldn't find any evidence of a crime. All that had happened was that someone had pushed the valves with a matchstick to let the air out. So Grandad had to get out there with a foot pump and pump the tyres up himself. I stood watching at the window with Nanna while she just tutted and shook her head, saying '*Jiw jiw*', which is Welsh for 'Good God'.

Chapter 8

The night-time visits continued to happen almost every night for the first few weeks. But things were about to get worse and the assaults were about to get a whole lot more serious.

Just before everything escalated, I remember a particular night that shocked me then and still shocks me now.

Grandad was in my room, groping around in the dark in his usual way, when I heard Nanna walking from their bedroom to the toilet across the landing. She had obviously noticed that Grandad was not in his bed, because after using the toilet, I heard her go downstairs, presumably to look for him. I heard her opening doors and softly saying

'Len?' as she checked each room. I even heard her open the back door momentarily, to check if he had gone outside.

After a couple of minutes, she came back up the stairs, walked along the landing and stopped outside my bedroom door. She was listening at my own door. My heart was pounding now. I felt sure there would be a terrible scene when Nanna found out what was going on. But, unbelievably, after standing and listening for a while, she said nothing at all, walked back to her own bedroom and apparently went back to bed.

Nanna said *nothing!* She said nothing even though she must have known he was in the room with me. Didn't she think that a little odd? Didn't she wonder what he was doing in there? It was like she was fine with it, almost as if she *expected* it!

I am convinced that what happened in the following weeks was partly down to Nanna's actions that night. Nanna had not said a word and had done nothing to stop him. So I think he took that almost as 'permission' to up his game. If she wasn't even going to object, then there was nothing now to stop him from intensifying the attacks.

It was very shortly later that Grandad raped me for the first time. He came into the room, pulled me from the bed, pushed me face down onto the bed so that I was bending over it. The feeling of that rough assault was horrific. I remember crying out in fear and pain. But he just put his big hand over the back of my head and pushed my face down into the bed to muffle my screams.

When he was finished he just got up and walked out of the room, leaving me lying face down on the bed. I curled up in bed and lay awake, horrified at what had just happened, for most of the night.

If Nanna didn't hear that first attack, she will certainly have heard the subsequent ones. Sometimes he was so rough that the walls shook and the bed squeaked. It was always from behind, pushing the side of my face or the back of my head into the bed. Almost like he couldn't bear to look me in the eye as he assaulted me.

I distinctly remember the next morning after that first attack because I didn't want to get out of bed. I had hardly slept and felt sick. I certainly didn't want to eat the huge breakfast that Nanna would have prepared. Most of all, I couldn't bear to face Grandad. I just felt so confused, so upset and so ashamed. How was I going to look him in the eye? Even at the age of eleven, I had had basic sex education at school and knew full well what he had done. Although no one had told me, I knew it was wrong.

But I was mostly ashamed by what I thought *I had done.* I thought that I had done something terribly wrong myself. I was a child who had 'had sex', and that was the worst thing a child could possibly do. I was deeply ashamed but also frightened about what trouble I would be in if someone found out. Would I be sent away? Perhaps put in care? Would I even go to prison? I never realised at such a young age that I had done nothing wrong whatsoever.

When Mum called that night, I felt ashamed to speak to her, like she could somehow tell what I had done.

'When can I come home, Mum?' I pleaded with her. She always answered in the same way. 'I have to get a little bit better first, then we can all be a big family again.' And she would always say, 'Are you being a good girl for your nanna and grandad?'

Chapter 9

It didn't happen every night. Sometimes, he would leave me alone and not visit my room. But I never knew whether he was coming or not. Because I never knew if tonight would be one of those nights, I would lie there wide awake for hours anyway, just waiting and praying. Only once I was sure they were both asleep would I let myself fall asleep. The only comfort about it being 'one of those nights' was that once Grandad had had his way and then left, I knew he wasn't coming again that night. That would allow me to sleep, and although I felt sick and upset, I knew I would then be safe until the next night. The worst of it was lying there in terror, just waiting and listening for his footsteps.

I slept so little that I was always still asleep when Nanna came to wake me in the morning. I often nodded off in the afternoon on the sofa because I was so tired.

I do remember one night when Grandad didn't come to my room, because I wasn't there for it to happen. I was to spend a precious night away from that terrible place, with the lovely Mrs Evans.

Once a year some organisation in the village would have a ball and Nanna and Grandad would dress up in black tie and a ball gown and rub shoulders with all the supposed great and good of the town. I only knew about this because I was staying there when the annual ball took place.

Nanna and Grandad got into their fancy clothes before dropping me at Mrs Evans's, who was going to babysit while they were at the ball. Nanna took all afternoon getting ready, fussing with her hair and putting her dress on and taking it off again to iron a bit of it that she thought looked wrinkly.

I clearly remember her dress was yellow. But Nanna never called it 'yellow'. It was always 'lemon'. That always used to annoy my mum – that Nanna would never say 'my yellow cardigan' but instead would always say 'my lemon cardigan'. Mum told me Nanna thought that was somehow posh, to wear lemon clothes rather than yellow clothes.

Nanna and Grandad went off to the ball, leaving me to stay at Mrs Evans's for the night. I had a fun night sitting on the sofa with Pushkin the Pekingese, who was allowed up on the furniture. Mrs Evans played with me and we watched an old film, *My Fair Lady*, on the television, eating snacks. I really liked Mrs Evans because she was kind and never said mean things about people like Nanna did. She only ever said nice things about Nanna, and I wondered what she would think if she knew about all the horrible things Nanna said about her.

Mrs Evans made up a bed for me on her big sofa, and Pushkin slept in the room with me. In the morning, she gave me crumpets and tea for breakfast. I was so happy there that when Nanna came to pick me up that morning, I didn't really want to go back with her.

'Can I stay another night, Nanna?' I pleaded with her? 'Mrs Evans is going to show me how to make pancakes.'

'It's alright with me, *bach*,' said Mrs Evans. ('*Bach*' is a Welsh word for 'dear'.) 'It's been lovely having her. I can give you a break another day if it's alright with you and Len.'

Nanna agreed. So I got to spend one more heavenly day and night with Mrs Evans, Pushkin the dog and loads of lovely pancakes. But the best thing about being at Mrs Evans's was that I could sleep peacefully on the sofa without any fear of a night-time visit from Grandad. I wished I could have stayed there the whole summer.

I remember coming back from Mrs Evans's to Nanna and Grandad's insufferably hot house, walking into the claustrophobic lounge with the ticking clocks, and my heart sinking. I just didn't want to be there. I so wanted to go home, or to Mrs Evans, or anywhere but that horrible hot house and that scary, scary Grandad.

But Nanna had lots to tell me that morning. She had been to the ball and had a whole night's worth of gossip to impart to me. And, of course, she used the ball as an excuse to boast even more than usual.

'Betty Morgan said to me, "This dress cost me eighteen pounds", and I said to her, "Is that all? Mine was twenty-five". And I showed her the receipt, there and then. Well, she didn't have a *word* to say to that!' she said proudly.

And then she took out her old photos, showing me all the photos of her and Grandad in previous years, explaining exactly what she was wearing in the photo and how much it had cost. The boasting continued all day.

'If you'd only *seen* the thing she was wearing! Like an old curtain. What a fright she looked! And can you believe her daughter's courting a black? Face as black as the ace of spades, it is. Imagine if there was a baby. Oh, the shame! If any daughter of mine carried on like that, I'd have her out the house!'

These were the sorts of things Nanna liked to talk about all the time. All the while boasting. All the while spouting vile racist comments and hate about other people while standing back and letting her own granddaughter be abused in her own house. Seriously, what sort of a grandmother does that? What sort of a *person* does that?

Even now, when I look back, I blame her just as much as him for what happened. I don't think to myself 'My grandad abused me'. I think 'My nanna and grandad abused me'.

In some ways, I have always been more angry and upset with Nanna than I was with Grandad. I think that's because I didn't expect any better from him. He was just a sick pervert, just a scary old man. It was easy to hate him.

The way I thought about Grandad was simple. I just despised the man.

But it was different with Nanna, because she was *my nanna!* How could she have done that? How could she stand back and let it just happen, without even saying a word? I just couldn't make sense of what had happened. I couldn't make sense of Nanna acting, or failing to act, in that way. She was supposed to love me. I had loved her too once upon a time. So in many ways, it has been far more difficult to deal with her betrayal than with his.

Chapter 10

Finally, the blessed day came. I was playing outside when Nanna called me from the garden and handed me the phone. It was my mother.

'Guess what, darling,' my mum said. 'The baby and I are all better now. He is out of hospital and I think it's time for you to come home and make friends with your new brother.'

I was so happy I started to cry on the phone.

'What's wrong, Emily?' she was confused. 'Don't you want to come home? Having too much of a good time on holiday with Nanna spoiling you, I suppose.'

Nothing could have been further from the truth.

'No, it's not that, Mum,' I said. 'I'm just really happy to be coming home again. Are you coming up today, right now?' I was hoping and praying she was going to say 'yes'.

'No, no, not now, love. Your dad will come up on Friday after work and bring you back. You'll be home for the bank holiday weekend. That'll be nice, won't it? We'll do something fun for it if the weather's nice. So just you be a good girl, pack your clothes and all your things. Don't make Nanna do it. And Dad will be up in a couple of days.'

I was so happy that day. I felt happy and free, like everything was going to be okay. Very soon, it would all be over and it was all going to stop. I would be going back to my own room where no one could hurt me. That was the best day since I got there. The happiest day of my stay at Nanna and Grandad's was the day I discovered I was going home.

But as the day wore on, a fear started to set in, a creeping feeling of dread. I just knew that night it would happen again.

And it was worse than usual. Grandad made me sit on the edge of the bed and ordered me to open my mouth. You can probably already guess what he did next. It was so awful; I could hardly stand it.

Then something happened that was to haunt me for years to come, something that changed the course of our family history. It was what happened next that was perhaps the greatest betrayal of all.

Grandad had his hand on the back on my head. He suddenly pushed a bit too hard and nearly choked me. That really scared me. I thought he might choke me to death if he did that again and I panicked. I twisted away from him and he momentarily dropped his grip on me. That was my chance, I had no choice but to call for help.

'Nanna! Nanna! Nanna!' I remember my voice sounding so high-pitched I was almost screaming. She would definitely have heard that.

Grandad looked at me with such fury, like he wanted to kill me. His finger went to his mouth, to make his usual *Shhhhhtttt!* noise to shut me up. But as he did so, we heard a movement from her bedroom. He just stopped, and looked up, as if listening for what would happen next. Footsteps in her bedroom. Thank God, Nanna was coming to help me at last. I relaxed a little. Nanna would sort it all out. Nanna would stop him. Nanna would protect me. Lovely Nanna.

Then I heard another sound, the unmistakeable sound of a door, *being shut!* Nanna had shut her bedroom door. She had shut the door on *me!*

She wasn't coming to help. She heard me cry out in terror for help, and she didn't even want to know. No one was coming. No one could help me. It was just me and my evil grandad, alone in that room. Then, Grandad spoke.

'What an inconsiderate little girl you are,' he said. 'Why would you want to wake your nanna like that? She has to be up at six to make the breakfast. Maybe think about that and try to be grateful, instead of bothering her.'

And then it all just got even worse. He became really pushy, choking me. And at that moment, I wondered if I might die in that room.

Eventually, it was over. Grandad let me go, and pulled up his pyjama bottoms. Then he spoke again. 'And don't you *dare* go telling stories and worrying your mam and dad about this. You don't want them to be upset, do you? Think about what it would do to them to hear your wicked little stories. Your dad would be so upset. If you tell your parents you'll get in terrible, terrible trouble because *no one will believe you*. You're not going to tell them, are you?'

I shook my head.

'Now, let's make a deal,' he said. 'You don't say a word to your mam and dad!'

I nodded. I would agree to anything. I wouldn't tell anyone. I just wanted to get away.

'You need to promise,' he said.

'I promise, Grandad.'

'That's not enough. I know what you girls are like, always lying and conniving.' Then he stopped and thought for a moment. 'You need to promise on your baby brother's life. If you break your promise to me, you'll be killing your baby brother.'

What could I do? I could hardly refuse. I was alone in a bedroom with him and my nanna had turned her back on me. I had to agree. That was the last time he ever came to my room.

A few days later, Dad came and picked me up, all smiles. He made me kiss Nanna and Grandad goodbye, and that was the end of this particular nightmare. It was the end of my abuse at the hands of my evil grandfather.

But it's not the end of the story.

Chapter 11

When I got home from Nanna and Grandad's there was a new baby in the house: my little brother, Marcus. He was safe home from hospital, having spent six weeks in an incubator. He was so tiny – the smallest person I had ever seen. His little toenails were like dots. He still had an oxygen tube in his nose all the time, helping him breathe. A jolly nurse would come to the house nearly every day to check him and change his tube. But other than that, Marcus was absolutely fine. He was tiny and his lungs were weak, but he was out of danger and was going to be okay. I thought he was the cutest thing in the world.

Marcus was a good baby and hardly ever cried. He was such a funny little boy and made us laugh so much. He seemed to smile at me from the day I met him, even though the health visitor said babies couldn't smile at that age, and that his smiles were 'only wind'. But what did she know? Marcus was my brother, and I knew that he was smiling at me.

We all loved him so much and it felt like a really happy time for all of us. It just didn't feel like the right time to tell anyone about Grandad. How could I do that to Mum and Dad after all they had been through. How could I ruin everything just as it had all started to feel good again. I so wanted to tell my parents everything, especially when, a few weeks later, they drove to Wales to let Nanna and Grandad meet Marcus. I couldn't stand the thought of Grandad holding my beautiful baby brother. But I knew that if I said something now, all that 'happy time' would be over.

Something strange happened shortly after Marcus was born. My two aunties, Sheila and Valerie, came from where they both lived in Manchester to visit for the weekend. At the time, I thought nothing of it and the memory is distant and not very clear. So it's only with hindsight that I now see the significance of that visit. It probably doesn't seem like there's anything remotely unusual about two aunties travelling hundreds of miles to visit their new baby nephew. And there wouldn't be anything unusual except that it didn't seem that they had come to see Marcus at all. From the moment they arrived, it seemed that they had come to visit *me.*

Dad had no brothers. His two sisters were much older than him and, although he always had nice things to say about them, he hardly ever saw them. I had only met them a couple of times. They never, ever visited Nanna and Grandad and apparently Auntie Val's two children had never even met their grandparents. Dad used to say his sisters had become estranged from the family because they didn't get on with Grandad.

So it was a bit strange that these two aunties, after having a brief cuddle with baby Marcus, made a beeline for me. At first, they started asking about normal things, like 'How's school?' and 'So what do you think of your baby brother?' But it soon became clear that all they really wanted to know about was my trip to Wales.

Sheila was in the kitchen talking to Dad and I was on my own on the couch with Auntie Val. The memory is quite vague so I can't remember the exact words. But the conversation went something like this.

'So, Emily, I hear you had a trip to stay with your nanna and grandad. Did you enjoy yourself?'

'Yes, thanks.' (That's the way you're taught to answer any grownup's question in a polite way.)

'So how was your nanna?'

'Fine, thanks.'

'Did she make you eat cake six times a day,' she joked.

'Yes!' I laughed a bit. 'But I didn't mind. I love cake.'

'And where did you sleep? Were you in my and Sheila's old room?'

'Yes.'

Silence.

'Have they still got the big old bed with the big bed-knobs?'

'Yes, and flowery wallpaper.'

Silence.

'Emily, did your grandad ever come in the room? You know, at night?'

This wasn't the time. I wasn't ready to talk. She may have been my auntie, but I hardly knew the woman. I hadn't even told my sister yet. And what about that promise I made on Marcus's life not to tell? No, this wasn't the time.

'I don't think so, Auntie Val.'

'Are you sure, Sweetie? You can tell your auntie, you know. You can tell me and Auntie Sheila anything. Are you sure Grandad never came to your room?

'No, Auntie.'

I don't remember much else about that visit. All I do know is that Val and Sheila were really kind to me that weekend and I liked having them there.

It must seem obvious to you now what Val was getting at, what the implications of her chat with me were, and why she was asking those questions. But this seemingly insignificant and vague memory only came back to me recently, a long time after the turn of events that I am about to explain to you.

Chapter 12

That promise that I had made to Grandad, swearing on Marcus's life, really shook me up. On one level I knew that it was all nonsense. You can't kill someone by breaking a promise. If I told Mum and Dad about Grandad, that could have no effect on Marcus whatsoever.

But on the other level, I used to worry, 'Was it really worth the risk?' What if somehow breaking a promise *could* affect someone else? I was a strong Christian when I was a little girl and I believed absolutely in the power of God. And who knows what He would do if I broke my promise. Maybe God would kill baby Marcus, just as a punishment to me.

In the Bible He had killed hundreds of people who broke His laws.

It was night-times when that promise would come back and haunt me. When my mind was all fuzzy my thoughts would go haywire. I'd have sort of waking dreams about telling Mum and Dad about what happened at Nanna and Grandad's, and Marcus immediately beginning to choke and dying there in front of us. Or I'd dream I'd go to his cot and find him all cold and blue. I'd lie there with tears streaming down my face, and just force the thoughts away. When that happened, I knew I couldn't tell Mum and Dad. I just couldn't because I had promised not to, on the life of my baby brother.

But I didn't promise not to tell Pauline.

I haven't said much yet about my older sister, Pauline. Pauline was a bit older than me, at thirteen. But throughout my childhood she seemed like a grown-up to me. She appeared to be as adult as Mum or Dad. I really looked up to her and she was very protective of me. We didn't have one of those relationships where sisters squabble and fight and are jealous of each other. We were friends and we loved each other.

When we were at primary school together, she really used to look after me. By the time Marcus was born, we were already in different schools. She'd left Westdean primary, where I still went, to go to St Margaret's High School. Our two schools were only about 200 metres apart, and every day after school Pauline would come out of St Margaret's and walk straight to the gates of my school to meet me and walk me home. While all her teenage friends must have been hanging out and gossiping about boys after school, Pauline was going to pick up her little sister. That's the sort of girl she was. The truth was Pauline was my best friend at that time. And we were soon to become closer than ever. It was unthinkable that I wouldn't tell Pauline about what had happened.

It was around four months or so before I told her. I know that because I remember there were Christmas decorations in the house. We shared a bedroom at that time, with two single beds alongside each other. We had a tiny plastic Christmas tree with lights on, sitting on the little table between the beds. My bedtime was 8 o'clock and Pauline came up a bit later at around 9. Very often, I was asleep by the time she came to bed and I usually didn't notice her come in. But one night, I hadn't fallen asleep straight away and was still awake when Pauline came up. I heard her get into bed, and after about 20 minutes I could tell she was still awake.

'Em,' she whispered. 'You still awake?'

'Yes, I can't sleep.'

'Me neither.'

Silence.

'Marcus was so funny today when he was laughing at Dad, wasn't he?'

'Yeah, he's so cute.'

'Dad says he looks just like Grandad. Who do you think he looks like?'

Silence. I didn't speak. It made me feel ill to think about Grandad and baby Marcus in the same moment.

'Emily? I said…'

'Yeah, I know. I just don't want to think about Grandad, that's all.'

'Why not?'

'I don't like Grandad much. Or Nanna.'

'Why?' And she sat up in bed and looked at me through the half-dark room.

And that's when I told her. I didn't go into all the horrible details like I have told you. I just told her that Grandad had come into my room at night and made me do terrible sex things. I told her that Nanna knew but she didn't stop him. I told her I even screamed out *Nanna, Nanna, Nanna!* But that Nanna had just shut her door on me, and never came to help.

'Emily,' she whispered through the darkness.

'Yes?'

'I always hated Grandad.'

I loved Pauline so much. I knew she would understand. I knew she would take my side. I knew she would believe me completely, without even stopping to think about it.

'Do you think we should tell Mum and Dad?' I asked.

'Do you want to tell them?'

'I don't know.'

More silence. Then Pauline spoke.

'I think you should definitely tell them. But not yet. Wait until after Christmas. Maybe wait until Marcus is a bit bigger.'

'But I promised on Marcus's life not to tell them.'

More silence.

'So *I'll* tell them instead,' said Pauline suddenly. 'I didn't promise anything to anyone! Then you won't have broken any promises at all!'

I knew she'd say all the right things. It felt really good to talk to someone about it. It felt really good knowing that we were going to tell Mum and Dad. And it felt really good knowing we weren't going to tell them *yet*.

Chapter 13

Christmas came. It was Marcus's first one and it was so lovely. Dad had bought a new camera just so he could take lots of pictures of us celebrating. I look back at those photos today into the eyes of the eleven-year-old me, hiding that terrible secret. There is a photo of all of us, all cuddled up with Marcus on the sofa with the Christmas tree in the background. Everyone is laughing and happy, but even then you can see the sadness, a lost look in my eyes.

Marcus had loads of presents for his first Christmas even though he was too tiny to even play with most of them. We had a special bauble made to put on the Christmas tree for him, with a picture of his face and his name and the date. All these years later, Mum and Dad still put that bauble on the tree every year.

But on the sideboard was a big 'Baby's First Christmas' card from Nanna and Grandad. I remember it had a picture of some sort of cute cartoon animal, a teddy or an elephant with a big head who was posting letters in the snow. That was the fashion back then – animals with huge heads. Always the biggest card in the shop. Always the biggest card on the sideboard. When I was very little I thought Nanna always bought the biggest card in the shop because she loved us so much. As an adult I realise it wasn't done out of love. She bought the biggest card so she could talk about it and make other people feel bad. She never would have realised that that card even made me feel bad every time I saw it. I hated to see it there and I tried not to look at it. It made my heart sink every time I caught a glimpse of it. When no one was looking, I laid it flat down on its face and put other cards on top of it. But Mum noticed and put it back up.

New Year came and went. We went back to school. Life just went back to normal. Months went by and still Pauline and I hadn't told anyone about Grandad. But we sometimes talked about it, just lying there in bed. We would always finish the conversation deciding to 'tell them soon', and then we would just go to sleep. It became sort of 'our thing' – we called it simply 'the Secret'. It was like an unspoken matter between us that we both thought about all the time, but only ever spoke about in private.

'You know the Secret?' I'd sometimes say as we were lying there. 'Why did he do it? Do you think he hates me?'

'No, he's just sick in the head. He's a bit mental, that's all,' she'd reply.

Or one of us would say, 'You know the Secret? Why do you think Nanna let him do it?'

'You know the Secret? Do you think Grandad will go to prison?'

'You know the Secret? I wonder if he's done it to anyone else?'

I think it was talking to Pauline that stopped me from going off the rails. I don't know what state I'd have been in if I hadn't had her to confide in. I know that other girls have suffered a lot worse than me after being abused. I did suffer, and I think I did go a bit crazy for a while. But I am sure that having Pauline to talk to made everything better. I think things would have gone very badly for me if Pauline had not been around.

It was Christmas again before she and I realised it had been a whole year and we still hadn't mentioned the Secret to Mum and Dad.

Pauline was now fifteen and wanted her own room. She was to have the little spare room to herself and I was to stay in the big room with the two single beds. Pauline was picking out wallpaper to make the little room her own. She was to have pale blue wallpaper with little white clouds all over it, pale blue curtains to match and a new duvet cover. I loved the wallpaper. I was a bit sad about her leaving me to sleep all alone. We had slept in the same room for as long as I could remember. But Pauline told me she would still come and sleep in our old room sometimes, if I felt lonely or scared. She was such a brilliant sister. She also promised we would tell Mum and Dad about Grandad before she moved rooms. It was our big plan, we were finally going to tell everyone about our evil grandparents.

And then it happened…

I came home from school to find Mum crying and Dad with his head in his hands. Oh God! What was wrong? Something terrible had happened, I knew it. I felt the terror rise in me. Was it Marcus? I looked around the room. No, Marcus was playing happily in his playpen, standing up to smile when he saw me come in the room. Thank God! What then? What was wrong? Was it Pauline? Please, please, don't let it be Pauline!

'Emily, come and sit down, Chickie.' (Mum always called us Chickie or Chick.) 'I've got some very sad news. Your grandad is very ill. He has cancer.'

Oh God, *is that all?* I flopped into a chair, weak with relief. It was only Grandad. Grandad had cancer, that's all. It's an awful thing to say, but I was *glad.*

At the age of 62, Grandad had got cancer of the throat. After a whole lifetime of smoking, it was hardly surprising that cancer would catch up with him in the end. But of course, this news meant I couldn't follow through with my plan. How could I tell Dad about what had happened now? After all, Grandad was *his* dad. I would have been devastated to know my dad had cancer, so how could I tell him his own father was a monster, just when he was about to lose him? I just couldn't do it. I couldn't come out and tell my parents that Grandad had abused me, while everyone was so upset. And even though I hated him, it just didn't feel right to accuse a dying man of such a terrible crime, even if he was completely guilty.

Chapter 14

So the Secret remained a secret and the years went by, while Grandad carried on living. He lived a further six years after being diagnosed with throat cancer. And I always wondered, why did *he* manage to be one of those who responded well to treatment? Why did *he* go into such a long remission? Why did *he* turn out to be a cancer treatment success story? Sometimes I used to think it was his nastiness and his stubbornness that kept him alive.

Of course, it was a terrible shame that Grandad was going to die so young. Everyone said so. 'He's young. He's such a great man. Why should he die when there are so many awful people still living? Why him?' That's the story that was told amongst all the family. But that's not what I was thinking. I was thinking, 'Why should he get to be the one that lives for six more years when my friend's mum died of breast cancer within a year?'

I still thought about what had happened all the time. And I did go a little crazy for a while and started acting up for Mum and Dad. I remember I sulked a lot and locked myself in the bedroom. I would lose my temper and throw things sometimes.

I can't remember the thoughts that led me to act like this. I only know that all this behaviour started almost immediately after coming back from Nanna and Grandad's. So it must have been a kind of reaction to all that trauma. I can't remember thinking about the injustice of it all, or feeling shame or disgust. I think I just kind of 'internalised' everything and that's why the feelings came out in my bad behaviour and moods. Sometimes, when I felt the most disgust, I would feel sick and would refuse to eat for a day or two. I eventually went on to develop anorexia and bulimia that was quite serious at one point.

The bulimia all started because I'd sometimes think about the Secret when I was eating a meal. And I would immediately feel sick. If I thought about it when I'd eaten a big meal, I felt so sick I'd sometimes throw up. So I just stopped eating big meals. Then I noticed how much better I felt when I had no food inside me. When I was full of food, I felt somehow dirty and disgusting. I felt fat and sick and horrible. But when I was empty of food, I felt clean and sort of 'pure'. I soon came to hate the feeling of food in my stomach. I would look at my body in the mirror and swear I could see the food poking through the wall of my tummy. And I'd feel disgusting when I saw that. It was so easy just to go to the toilet, stick my finger in my mouth and stroke the back of my throat, and throw everything up. Then I would feel empty and clean again. That was how the bulimia started. I came to prefer the feeling of hunger to the sight of my fat stomach with food in. So I began to eat less and less and get thinner and thinner.

I'm a lot better now because I got help for my bulimia, but often these eating disorders never really go away. I'm always painfully aware of how much I'm eating, and although I do eat properly and no longer vomit, I never let myself feel 'full'. It is still with me to this day to some extent and I'm always officially 'underweight'.

Throughout all of this, I always had Pauline. When I refused to eat for days on end, she didn't try to force me, or tell me I was going to die of malnutrition, like Mum and Dad always did. She just quietly would say, 'Just eat a little bit and they'll leave you alone. Here, have that little bit of chicken and one potato. Then they'll stop hassling you.' She was sometimes the only one who could get me to eat.

I could go on for ages, telling you all about the eating disorder and the doctors and the clinic I had to attend to get over the problem. But I'm not going to do that. I want to stop identifying myself as a bulimic and I don't think it does me any good to keep telling the story. I know I'm still too thin and I don't want to end up teaching my children the same bad habits. So let's just stop talking about the bulimia for now.

That wasn't the only emotional problem I had in those years after the attacks. I also started to behave really badly for Mum and Dad. Perhaps I would have ended up being a bad kid anyway, even without Grandad. But I doubt it. I do remember being a really happy child. And I remember when I started to become really unhappy and angry all the time.

Whenever I acted out, sulking or losing my temper, it was Pauline who always understood exactly what was going on. Even when I was really losing it, throwing things or shouting, she was the one who was always able to calm me down. She would just come over, take my hand and pull me upstairs or to the garden, sit me down and just be there for me while I calmed down. She didn't sit in front of me and stare at me like everyone else always did. It's so stressful when someone does that, just looking at you straight in the eyes, all expectantly, waiting for you to do something. Pauline never did that. She would sit by the side of me, facing the same way as me so I could just calm down in my own time, without the pressure of someone staring at me. But it was still nice to have someone there with me. Sometimes she didn't even say anything. Just her being there was enough. I knew that she knew, and that was what I needed. We would just sit in silence until my panting and panicking slowed.

I can't even begin to imagine how life would have turned out for me if I hadn't had Pauline. I know that some children have to go through the same abuse as I did, and yet have no one to talk to, no one to tell, no one to be there for them when they lose their shit. It scares me even to think of what they must be going through. Poor, poor children. Pauline definitely saved my sanity. She might even have saved my life.

As we grew into teenagers, things changed between us. She got a rubbish boyfriend, split up with him, and then got a good one. They got engaged. And we both got part-time jobs. There was so much to take up our time in those years. When she was around twenty years old, Pauline moved out of the family home and in with Keith, her fiancé.

We were still friends, of course, but it was never the same as when we were little children, sharing secrets in that shared bedroom. I know it sounds crazy but I still miss those times even now. I think those nights when Pauline and I would sit up and talk until midnight were the times in my life when I felt safest.

Chapter 15

I was eighteen when Grandad's cancer stopped responding to all treatment. He was going to die, and this time, even he couldn't escape it. When it was clear his time was near, plans were being made for a huge, fancy funeral. I would hear Mum and Dad talking about it in the evenings, while they thought I was watching television. They always spoke in hushed voices, as if I was eight, not eighteen. And as if I couldn't still hear every word they said, being in the same room.

Nanna, in her usual way, was planning to have the biggest and grandest funeral ever. She was planning to hire out a room in the town hall and have fancy caterers walking around with silver platters. She wasn't going to have any ordinary black hearse either. Grandad's coffin was to be carried in a glass carriage pulled by black horses with feathers on their heads.

'They'll be talking about it for years,' she had apparently boasted.

Dad wasn't very happy about any of this. He just wanted to have a quiet affair. But she wouldn't hear of it.

'She's going to ruin herself with this flipping funeral,' he said. 'I think she cares more about what the neighbours think than whether he lives or dies.'

Nanna wanted everyone to remember that she had been married to a very 'great man'. She was petitioning to have a plaque erected at the school where he taught and even inside the church. She had also wangled her way to getting a tree planted in the churchyard in his name. Grandad needed to make sure everyone continued to know just what a 'great man' he had been, even after he died.

Grandad always used to say that streets would be named after him when he died. It seemed vitally important to him that he be remembered, honoured in death. He would talk about ancient myths where the hero lived on after his death through his legacy. He often used to say that those who die without a proud legacy have wasted their lives.

So Grandad's legacy would live on, just as he wanted. Nanna would make sure of that. She would be the poor grieving widow. And she would love it, basking in the sympathy, the admiration, the jealousy of others. It was all she had ever lived for. She would continue to be Mrs Wilkins, widow of the late, great Len Wilkins, pillar of the community, churchwarden, beacon of respectability. She would be guest of honour at his various memorial occasions, sitting, dabbing away a fake tear with a lace handkerchief embroidered with his initials. I bet she couldn't wait for him to die.

But as these preparations went on, my resentment started to grow. First it was just irritating to hear the bigger and yet grander plans for the funeral of this 'very great man'. But as time went on, the anger grew until I began to seethe. How could I let this happen? How could I let this hateful pervert be honoured in such a way?

It had been years since I had seen either of them, having conveniently found desperately important reasons for not visiting them time and time again. I was then eighteen years old and grown-up enough to make excuses for not visiting my grandparents.

I don't remember how long it was before I heard the news. Grandad was dying. Doctors had stopped all treatment and he was only going to be given painkillers until he died. He was expected to last only a few weeks. I hadn't seen him in years and I had no intention of changing that now. When all the rest of the family drove up to pay their respects to the dying man, I refused to go. They all went up to Wales without me. But when they returned they put enormous pressure on me to visit him, on my own, if necessary.

'You *must* go and see him, Emily,' insisted my mother. 'You'll come to regret it if you don't. I know he's a silly old man but he was very kind to you when you were little and went to stay with him.' And then she added, 'Dad will be so upset if you don't say goodbye to him. Can't you do it for your dad?'

This time, there were no excuses that were going to cut it. I had no choice if I was not to upset my own father, who had never done an unkind deed in his life. I had to go and say goodbye to my evil grandfather.

Once the decision was made, I no longer tried to put off the visit. I needed to get this over with as soon as possible. Even so, every day leading up to my visit I would pray that he would die before I got there. Every time the phone rang my heart would beat faster and I would be silently praying for the 'bad' news. But deep down I knew that call would never come. Grandad was far too stubborn to die early. He would do his utmost to outlive the doctors' predictions, even if by just one day. Just to show them he knew better.

Chapter 16

I decided to drive to Nanna and Grandad's house by myself, having very recently passed my driving test. I had managed to persuade Mum to let me take her car for the trip. I knew the fact I was going at all was a bargaining point and that she was bound to say yes to my taking the car.

I had woken up very early that day, with a feeling of dread. I knew this was the last time I was ever going to see my grandfather. This was my chance to say whatever I had to say to the man who had raped me as a child, stolen my childhood, led me into a serious eating disorder and panic attacks, and left me a nervous wreck.

The whole way my stomach was churning and I had to stop loads of times to go to the toilet. Nerves always gave me a bad tummy and diarrhoea. As I crossed the Clifton Suspension Bridge, I started to feel a rising fear. The horrible thought crossed my mind that I might have a full-blown panic attack, here on the bridge. I'd never considered suicide before, but right there and then on the bridge, it was all I could do to resist stopping the car and flinging myself off.

But I'd never have done that. I would never do that to my family, to my mum and dad and to Pauline. They had done nothing wrong whatsoever, and they didn't deserve that. And besides, I told myself, I was only going to spend five minutes with a dying man. It would be over in no time. I could cope with that after all this time. I started my deep breathing exercises that I used whenever things got on top of me. And I started to feel a bit better. I was over the worst of the panic now, and I knew I'd be okay again soon. I stopped at the Gordano services for a cup of tea and to calm down. It had changed a lot. I thought back to how much I used to love this place, how exciting I found it, with all the arcade games and the brightly lit shop selling magazines and travel games. Then I remembered the time that

Dad brought me on my own, and bought me fish and chips before leaving me at Nanna and Grandad's. Gordano services just didn't feel the same any more, having become forever connected to the Secret.

It was another couple of hours' drive after the bridge to Nanna's house in mid-Wales. I drove the whole way trying not to think of anything at all. I just practised my Welsh pronunciation as I read all the foreign-sounding place names written on the signs I passed. Finally, I saw the sign for their village.

I turned the corner into my grandparents' street, stopped the car outside and just sat there for a few minutes, looking at their house. Same plastic red roses in a vase in the window. Same net curtain with a shire horse and a ploughing scene. Nothing had changed. *Nothing.* Eventually, I summon up the courage to do this thing, to start the ordeal, to get it over with. Same ding-dong doorbell. The light went on in the hall and the broad shape of Nanna appeared through the wobbly glass of the front door.

'Oh Emily, *bach*!' she said as the door opened. 'I'm so glad you came. It's been such a trying time for me. My nerves are up and down. I haven't had a moment's rest in a month and the nurse only comes for an hour a day to help. I swear I'll faint away from the stress of it all. But now you're here, you can help your old nanna.'

I thought this was about him? I thought.

It was the first time I had been back in years. But once again, as I walked through the hall into the insufferably hot lounge I thought *Nothing has changed*. I sat on the fat flowery sofa and looked around the room. The gas fire was on full. Pictures of crying kids and puppies. Horse brasses. Hideous windmill painting above the mantelpiece. Ticking clocks. Too, too hot.

Nanna made tea and offered me sponge cakes dipped in coconut. It was vaguely touching that she remembered they were my favourite. But since the bulimia kicked in I hardly ever eat cake any more, thanks to her and Grandad. I ate the cake out of politeness but my mouth felt so dry, it was like eating ashes or dust. I had to drink lots of tea just so I could swallow.

I balanced my bone china teacup and saucer and the plate of cake on my knee, trying not to spill my tea or drop crumbs. But I was eighteen, an adult. I suddenly felt defiant, sulky. And then I thought *fuck it!* And I put the teacup and saucer down on the floor with a clatter. Nanna's eyes widened in shock and disapproval. But I didn't care. I was a grown woman, and she was protecting a filthy child rapist. I forced down the last bit of cake, brushed the crumbs off my lap onto the carpet, and put the plate on the floor too. She probably couldn't believe my appalling manners. I could just see her thinking *What would the neighbours think?*

I *so* didn't give a shit. What was she going to do? Purse her lips at me? Tut-tut at me? There was a child rapist lying upstairs, but all that paled into insignificance compared to… *cake crumbs on the carpet!* Yeah, go ahead, Nanna. Do your worst. Tut at me. That will teach me!

Now that I had defied her, finally, I felt braver. I no longer felt afraid in this house. I couldn't believe just a couple of hours earlier I had thought of suicide. I had the bolshiness of a teenager, but with newfound resilience. I had found some strength. I had found some power.

And I would get my revenge.

'Come on then, Nanna. Let's get this over with. Where is the old fucker?' I said suddenly.

Nanna actually gasped and then looked at me

in disbelief. Then she was all of a fluster. I'd never spoken like this in front of her. She didn't purse her lips together or tut. She just opened her mouth and closed it.

I ignored her and walked off to find him. Up the stairs, along the passageway to his room. But on opening the door, I found an empty bed. Where was he? And then I realised.

Oh God, they'd put him in the spare room! In *my* room. He was in the very room he abused me in. He was lying in the bed where he abused his eleven-year-old granddaughter.

Chapter 17

As I walked in I saw that same ugly jug and basin that was there all those years ago, that I once thought was so posh. And I couldn't believe I once loved that rose-covered wallpaper. And in *that bed* lay my grandad. He was lying there dying in the *Princess and the Pea* bed. In the *Bedknobs and Broomsticks* bed. I had to say goodbye to him in the very room in which he abused me. In the very *bed* in which he abused me!

Grandad had always wanted to breathe his last at home, in bed. I could only imagine that in order to make things easier for Nanna to care for him, they had made the spare bedroom into a makeshift hospital room for him.

I just stood in the room and looked down at him. He was thinner than a stick. Like a skeleton with skin on, like those people in old news films about Jewish death camps. There were deep hollows on either side of his skull where there were no bones and the skin seemed to have been sucked inwards. I'd never seen a person so thin in real life. He had a tube in his nose, and an oxygen tank by the bed, just like Marcus did when he was a baby. His breathing was like gasps, but with a horrible rumble like his chest was full of nasty stuff.

He looked at me with obvious recognition, but said nothing. He was too weak and breathless to speak. His eyes looked wet and slimy, like they were covered in watery glue.

I felt not one ounce of sorrow or sympathy. I had no desire to kiss him or hold his hand. In fact, I felt myself hardening as I stood and looked at him. For a moment I worried that I might soften, give in, and feel sorry for him. So I remained stony faced and stony hearted. I needed to make sure no kindly feelings had a chance of seeping out of me. I hated him so much.

I sat in the chair opposite for a while, just watching him. I thought of everything that had happened since those attacks. I thought of the fear and the panic, and the bulimia and the promise he made me make on my baby brother's life. I thought of the feelings of revulsion and shame. I thought of how different life could have been if only I had never come to stay. I thought of how he had robbed me of my fun and happy childhood.

I was seething with bitterness and injustice. I'd never felt hatred like this before, and it made me brave. I wanted to hurt him, to hit him and punch him in the stomach. I wanted to smash his face in and kick him in his shrivelled up old balls.

There was a cushion on the chair I was sitting on, the potty chair. I picked up the cushion and looked at it. Then I looked at him. He knew what I was thinking. Thirty seconds and he'd be dead. He just barely found the strength to shake his head. I put the pillow down. No, that wasn't my plan. I had no desire to murder him. But I was happy to have scared him for a moment. No, my plan was far worse. Sitting there, I'd thought of a better plan. I'd thought of the best revenge ever.

'I'm going to tell them, Grandad,' I said simply. 'I'm going to tell them all what you did. I'm going to stand up at your funeral and tell the whole town. Everyone will know what you did.' The hatred was pouring out of me now. 'They'll all know what you are. Len Wilkins the pervert.' He didn't say a word. But his eyes were wide now.

'You're going to have a legacy, Grandad. But I'm going to tell it, and you won't be around to defend yourself. You're going to be hated and humiliated and shamed. But you'll already be dead, Grandad. You won't be around to fight back.'

And then I said nastily, 'No one's going to remember you as a great man, Grandad. They'll forever talk about you as Len Wilkins the kiddie-fiddler. Len Wilkins the paedophile. *They'll talk about this for years*.'

It felt so good to say it. I felt so free. I felt so pumped up and excited, saying all these horrible things. Does that make me a terrible person?

I didn't care. At that moment, I just didn't care about anything but hurting my Grandad as hard as I could, just like he had hurt me.

His breathing had become really fast and he looked horrified. He tried to say something but couldn't get the words out. He raised his hand to me and started to choke a little bit and I wondered for a moment if he was just going to die here in the room in front of me. I had no desire to see him die. Not because it would upset me, but just because I couldn't be bothered to deal with the messiness of it.

I didn't want to be there waiting for doctors and ambulances. I didn't want the fuss of people asking about it, of having to talk about it in a pretend concerned way. No, I wanted to be far, far away when he finally croaked. I got up to go.

'Goodbye and good riddance, you bastard,' I said as I left the room.

I went down to the lounge, picked up my bag and shouted to Nanna who was in the kitchen. 'I'm off then, Nanna!'

'But…' she came out of the kitchen, protesting. 'I thought you were going to stay and help me? I can't manage your Grandad and all the housework. And Mrs Evans is coming over tonight and I haven't got any bread in for the sandwiches. *Emily, I need your help!*'

I just looked at her, incredulous. I put my head on one side as if to say *Really? YOU need help, Nanna? YOU need help? Where were you when I needed help? Where were you when I was in danger, Nanna?*

And I did exactly what she did to me, when I called out in the night all those years ago. I turned around, walked away and I *shut the door on her!*

See you at the funeral, Nanna.

Chapter 18

And here I am, at Grandad's funeral, about to do it. I'm going to stand here, at my grandad's funeral and tell everyone the truth. The church is full. I walk up to the lectern. I am shaking from head to foot. I have a piece of paper in my hand with a speech, telling a story of a kindly grandfather, who I respected and looked up to, who taught me maths and told me about politics. But I'm not going to read that. No, I'm finally going to tell the truth.

Grandad died three weeks and one day after being told he had three weeks to live. It was a bit of an anti-climax when it happened. Nanna had called the house and asked to speak to Dad and apparently said, 'I think your dad's died'. But she wasn't actually sure. Dad jumped in the car immediately and drove up to Wales. For hours I didn't know whether Grandad was dead or alive so when we finally got the call that he had actually passed away, it wasn't a shock or a surprise.

Dad has been very quiet ever since it happened, but he hasn't cried. He's just very distant and doesn't seem to have much to say. Today, the day of the funeral, I haven't heard him say a single word.

As I walk to the lectern, I pass Nanna who is sitting in the front pew, as she always did. She's dressed immaculately in a black brocade twinset and a new hat with a black veil, perfectly perched on her freshly coiffed hair. She has a black silk rose pinned to her lapel, and she's dabbing her eyes affectedly with a black hanky. And I think *Where the hell did she find a black hanky?*

I climb the stairs of the lectern. Four steps. Only four. I actually count them as I go up and wish there were more. At the top I stop and look at the faces of the congregation.

Finally, I'm going to tell them all…

…and I open my mouth to speak.

And then I catch sight of my dad, looking up at me. And he's crying! My big burly dad is crying! I've never seen him cry before and it breaks my heart to see. His eyes are red and he's shaking a bit, but he's got a smile on his face as if to say, 'That's my girl!'

All the hate in me melts away. It was the hate that made me brave. And I just can't feel hate while watching the pitiful scene of this big bear of a man crying over the loss of his father. And then I know I can't do it. I can't do it to him. I can't stand up and upset my dad who has never done a thing wrong in his life. I can't embarrass my whole family. I can't do it to any of them. This day is not about me. It's not for me. It's not really even for Grandad. It's for the family that are left behind. Yes, Nanna is a bitch. She deserves the shame, it's true. But Nanna isn't the only one sitting out there in the pews. There are also my aunties, Sheila and Valerie. There is my dad, and all the cousins. Much as I want to humiliate Grandad on his deathbed, I know the day is about the people left behind as much as it is the dead man.

I look down at my piece of paper with the empty words, and I start to speak. I tell a story about a loving grandfather who used to read me Dickens and teach me maths. I tell a tale of a great man, who will be sadly missed. The words may be empty of feeling, but they are respectful and appropriate. I don't offend anyone. I do my duty. Nothing will change. There will be no scene. I will keep my mouth shut for the good of everyone else.

I finish speaking, close the piece of paper and turn to walk down the four steps. I go back to my seat in the church, without looking at anyone. I can't bear to see their smiling looks of admiration for the speech and thanks for the kind words. I have a sinking feeling in my stomach. The tears are now falling and I don't have a hanky. I have to wipe my eyes on my sleeves.

I feel small, sick and desperately disappointed. I have failed. I have protected my family from shock and shame. But I have failed myself. I have shamed myself. No one will ever know now, I think. I might as well just keep this Secret safe, for the good of everyone concerned. This isn't just about me. I'm not the only one that's important here. It will remain my dirty little Secret forever.

But it's going to get worse. The main event is about to start. Nanna is about to get up to speak. She's about to give the eulogy she's been writing for the last forty years. She's going to talk all about her vile husband as if he were Jesus Christ. She's going to talk of him being *a very great man.* She's going to talk about all his wonderful work done for the local community. She's going to talk about his first-class degree from Cardiff University. She's going to talk about him being head of department at the boys' school. She's going to talk about his commitment to the church. She's not going to mention his predilection for child rape. She's not going to mention how she's been complicit in his paedophilia.

I can't listen to this. I need to get out of this church. Now. I suddenly get up from my pew and, as quietly as I can, walk quickly up the side of the pews and leave the church. I'm half running by the time I get outside. No one will think it odd that I got up and walked out. They'll just think I have become overcome with grief.

They'll never know the truth now.

Chapter 19

I remember that day it was raining outside and I was glad. It was a warm summer rain and it felt fresh, cleansing. I walked over into the graves surrounding the church and stood under a yew tree growing among the gravestones. I was really crying now, sobbing uncontrollably. My nose was running with snot and I didn't have a hanky. Despite the comforting rain, I felt utterly desolate. I remembered that moment so clearly, because it was one of the lowest moments of my life. I felt hopeless, the deepest disappointment I have ever felt. It was as if nothing good could ever happen again.

I had only been standing there a few minutes when I saw someone else leaving the church. A woman. She opened an umbrella and started walking towards me. It was Pauline. Of *course*, it was Pauline!

She came over to me, stood close alongside and held the umbrella over both of us. She took out a packet of tissues and handed a wad of them to me so that I could blow my nose. She said nothing for a while, just like she used to do when we were kids and her presence alone was enough to calm me down. She just stood like she always does, side-by-side with me, looking out at the church from under the tree. Even now that we had drifted apart a little, I could still feel the sisterly feeling between us.

'You were going to tell them, weren't you?' she said, suddenly. Pauline always knew what was going on in my head. She knew what I was thinking, most of the time. I didn't say anything in reply for a while. Then I broke down.

'But I bottled it, Pauline! I bloody bottled it! I had all these things planned that I was going to say, and when I got up there, I saw Dad, and he was crying and I just couldn't. I couldn't do it to him. And now the old bastard's got away with it all. I just let him get away with it. I feel so weak. I'm such a failure.'

'What the fuck are you talking about, Em?' she said. 'Of *course* you couldn't do it there! Who the hell *could* stand up in a bloody church in front of all those people and say something like that? Fuck knows, *I couldn't,* that's for sure.' (Pauline always liked to swear a lot.) 'You're not a failure, Em,' she said. 'I think you're so brave for even planning to do it, for even *thinking about it.'*

She always said the right things.

'But Em, I just want you to know, that if you ever *did* want to say something, at any point, now or whenever, I'll be with you one hundred per cent. I'll tell them what you told me when it happened. I'll be right behind you to back up your story.'

'What's the point?' I said. 'What's it going to solve?'

'Look, that stupid old woman is about to turn that old bastard into some sort of national bloody hero. She'll be having fucking statues erected to him if we don't say something. Think about that. What's that going to be like? It will drive you bloody mental.'

'But what about Dad?' I said. 'It would kill him to know.'

'Yeah, but if it's killing *you* then what's the point? You can't go mad yourself just to protect Dad. We should have told everyone years ago. I'm sorry I let it get to this point without *making* you tell them. Today's not the time, I agree with that. But at some point, we are going to tell them. I promise you this time. No excuses. Both of us are going to tell them. Together.'

'Thanks, Pauline. I'm feeling a lot calmer and stronger now.'

She put her arm through mine and we stayed there for a while, just watching the rain on the ancient gravestones. Eventually, we noticed that people were beginning to leave the church. The funeral must have been over.

But we didn't walk to the graveside. Once upon a time, in rural Wales, women weren't allowed to attend funerals at all. When Grandad died, women did attend but they wouldn't go to the graveside. All the women would go back to make the tea and get everything ready for the wake, waiting like servants for the men to arrive back.

I hated this sort of old-fashioned sexist rubbish. Even then, I think this custom was dying out and it was only the more remote communities that still kept the tradition of keeping the women away. And if it had been anyone but Grandad, I would have insisted on going to the graveside. I wouldn't have let anyone tell me I couldn't, just because I was a woman. I'd make the men make their own bloody tea and tell them to get me a cup while they were at it.

But it *was* Grandad. And I had no desire to pay any respects at the grave of that horrible old man. I left that to my Dad.

Nanna was to be driven the two hundred metres to the town hall in a black hearse. As she came out of the church, Mrs Evans, Nanna's friend, and another Welsh lady were walking on either side of Nanna, holding her arms, as she fluttered and flustered about her heart and her nerves. They helped her into the car.

So Pauline, all the other women and I walked back to the town hall, while my Dad and the other men, the *important* men of the town, all went to see the coffin lowered into the ground. Keith, Pauline's boyfriend, came back with the women. I liked him for doing that.

I noticed that my aunties, Sheila and Valerie, Nanna's own daughters, were walking together, way behind us. They made no attempt to comfort Nanna or to help her. They hadn't even sat with her in church but had been way back in the pews near the door.

Nanna got into the waiting black car and was driven ahead of us to the wake. It was only a five-minute walk for the rest of us and most of us arrived at the same time as the car.

We entered the room at the town hall to find it full of flowers – vast elaborate arrangements of lilies. There were white linen tablecloths and a line of waiters and waitresses, standing to attention and waiting to serve us all. If I hadn't known otherwise, I'd have thought we were about to celebrate a wedding, not a funeral.

Almost as soon as she arrived at the wake, Nanna recovered from her grief and immediately was in the kitchen area of the hall, telling the caterers how to do their job – how to arrange the food and at which angle to lay the napkins across the plates. I heard her asking whether they had polished the cutlery.

The room was full of women – my mum and sister, the aunties, Mrs Evans and all the women townsfolk were standing around.

And then something amazing happened.

Nanna came out of the kitchen, heels clicking on the parquet floor. She was all in a bother.

'I told them John West salmon sandwiches. I clearly told them that. Well, I've seen the tin in the bin and it's ordinary salmon from the *Cash and Carry.* Can you believe it? I told them, I know they probably aren't used to doing events of this importance, and they aren't from 'round here so they don't know just whose funeral this is. But I told them straight. "This is no ordinary funeral. That's Len Wilkins we've just buried," I told them. "And Len Wilkins was a very *great man.*"' And then she added, 'This town will never see the like again!'

Then it happened. My auntie Valerie made a sort of half-laugh, half-snorting sound. As if she had just heard something totally unbelievable. Everyone turned and looked at her. What was *that* about?

'I'll thank you to have a little more respect, Valerie Jones!' said Nanna angrily (Jones was Auntie Val's married name).

'Oh, shut your mouth, Mam,' said Auntie Val.

Nanna pursed her nasty lips, and then said, 'You wash your mouth out! That's not the way you were brought up to act. What a thing to say at your own father's funeral. Ashamed of you, I am! Ashamed!'

Well that did it. It was Sheila who started the outburst.

'Ashamed, Mam? *You're ashamed of us?* While you stand there like butter wouldn't melt, knowing what he did. Knowing what sort of a man he really was? Knowing what he did to me and Val, every night, year after year!'

Sheila was really shouting now, shrieking at the top of her voice, like she wanted everyone in the hall to hear her.

'You know what, Mam?' she screamed. 'I *am* ashamed! I'm ashamed to be your daughter. I'm ashamed to be Dad's daughter. I'm ashamed to be at this funeral, all talking as if he was Nelson bloody Mandela. He wasn't a good man, Mam! He was a child molester!'

'Well, you lying little…' Nanna started. But Auntie Val cut her dead.

'Don't try and deny it, Mam,' Val said calmly. 'You know what he was doing to us at night. You knew it was happening. I tried to tell you but you'd never listen. I even saw you standing in the doorway while he was doing it, lots of times!'

The whole room was now almost silent. There were open mouths everywhere. Just a few of the women were speaking in tiny whispers. The catering staff were still moving about, but ever so slowly and quietly, as if they all wanted to hear what was coming next too.

'He did it to me, too.'

There were gasps everywhere. Everyone turned to look at me. And I realised: it was me speaking. I hadn't planned to say anything but it was like the voice was coming from somewhere deep inside.

'He did it when I came to stay, when Marcus was born,' I said. 'Nanna stood at the door and listened. Once I called for help, but she shut the door on me.'

Then it was Nanna's turn to lose it. She strode towards me in her two-inch heels and, raising her hand, slapped me hard across the face.

There were gasps everywhere, and squeals of *Jiw jiw!* from the ladies.

I don't remember exactly what happened in exactly what order after that. There was a huge commotion. I remember ladies pulling Nanna away because she was going to hit me again. I remember Sheila rushing over to me and giving me a hug so hard I thought she'd break my ribs. Val came to hug me too, and she was crying. Pauline appeared and she was crying too, but smiling at the same time.

Then Mum was screaming at Nanna, calling her a bitch and Nanna was screaming back, calling her a baggage and an unfit mother. Ladies were holding other ladies back from hitting each other.

It was, for all the world, like a big catfight.

Yes, Nanna. You got your wish. They remembered the funeral for years.

Chapter 20

It was all we spoke about for months. And for a while there was quite a lot of turmoil in the family because of what had gone on at Grandad's funeral. There were even some arguments between my mum and me. You see, Mum had been the peacemaker in the family and she always tried to see the good in everyone. She always really got on well with Nanna and looked to her as a sort of mother herself. (Mum's mum, Granny, had died when Mum was just a teenager.)

We had a really big argument where we both ended up in tears. Perhaps she felt a bit guilty for leaving me there with that monster. But I also think Mum just couldn't stand to believe what Nanna had done. I remember Mum trying to convince me that Nanna wasn't really to blame in any way, that she was just completely dominated by her husband, that things were different for women back then, that Nanna didn't really have a choice... and so on.

But I just couldn't bring myself to accept this. Over the years, the love I once had for Nanna had slowly evaporated. And now I hated Nanna for what she had done. So when Mum carried on defending Nanna I lost it with her.

'Mum, she *listened at the door!*' I shouted at her. Mum went quiet when I said that. She stopped trying to defend Nanna any more. And after that, I can't remember her ever speaking in her defence again.

Perhaps you think I'm being too harsh, too. Perhaps you agree with Mum. But as I see it, if a woman doesn't act to protect her own children and grandchildren from abuse, she might as well have done it herself. That's what I believe. Ask yourself, would *you* just lie in bed listening while your husband abused your daughters, your granddaughters?

No, I didn't think so.

As the years went on, we stopped talking about either of them. All the photos of them were taken down. I don't know if Mum and Dad still have photos, somewhere locked away. But if they do, they never bring them out.

As you might have expected, I became much closer to my two aunties, Sheila and Val. Just once, we three sat down and talked really frankly about everything that had gone on. Sheila, the eldest, said the abuse started when she was around twelve. But according to Val, it started so early that she couldn't even remember a time when Grandad wasn't visiting her room at night. The most shocking thing about their stories is that they shared a bed at the time. All three of them in the same room at the time the abuse was happening – can you imagine? Grandad would tell one of them to lie on her side and face the wall, while he assaulted the other.

Both of them assured me that Nanna knew very well what was going on. One time Val had confronted her mother about what her dad was doing, and this was Nanna's response: 'He's just being a man. You've got to let men be men.'

It had only stopped for Sheila when she had a pregnancy scare at the age of fifteen. Grandad left her alone from then on, but continued to abuse

Valerie until about the same age.

Why didn't they tell someone? A relative? The police? A teacher? The idea of telling someone in authority was unthinkable back then, my aunties told me.

'It was not like it is now,' Val said. 'These days, when a child reports abuse, everyone believes the child, not the abuser. But back then, people often took the side of the man.'

Val and Sheila told me the story of another girl, so shocking that it's hard for us to imagine today. Many years ago, there was a girl, Ivy Harris, who was a school friend of Sheila's. Poor Ivy became pregnant at the age of 16 after being attacked by a stranger on the recreation ground. They caught the man who committed the horrible crime, but he was let go with a warning. And as for poor Ivy, she was completely shunned by the community. No one would speak to her or be her friend. She was eventually sent away to some sort of home for 'disgraced women' to have her baby. She never returned. No one in the town seemed to know or care what had happened to her.

'But if you'd both have told the same story, they'd have to believe you,' I said. 'They'd have to have done something about it.'

'We thought about it,' said Val. 'But we were afraid that no one would believe that a respectable man like Grandad would have been capable of such a thing. They probably would have accused us of just making it up to get back at our dad or something. And you don't understand the shame we'd have felt, Emily. Even if they'd all believed us, our lives wouldn't have been worth living.'

No wonder my poor aunties never told anyone back then. It's not like they could run to their dad for protection from a dangerous man. Their dad *was* the dangerous man.

Chapter 21

But this was no longer the 1950s. And attitudes had changed lot since that time, thank God.

Shortly after the funeral, someone got into the school at night, smashed the trophy cabinet and crushed up the 'Maths Cup', the trophy that was named for Grandad. But there had been no sign of a break-in at the school, no smashed windows or crowbarred doors – someone had either been let in or got in with keys.

Everyone in the town knew it had been done by a group of dads, they even knew who did it. The group apparently included the caretaker, Wally Holt, and David Jones, the neighbour that Grandad embarrassed in front of his own little boy. The police did investigate but they seemed hardly interested in pursuing it. Wally Holt got someone to give him an alibi, and the rest of the community closed ranks and didn't say a word when the police asked for witnesses. With so little evidence and with nothing else stolen or damaged but this one paedophile's trophy, the police were happy to let the matter go. It wasn't really surprising. After all, most of them were fathers too.

We didn't get the police involved to investigate the abuse. There was no point. Nanna and Grandad had already had the worst punishment possible. They were now despised and reviled by the whole town as criminals, as paedophiles. Even the gypsies would spit at Nanna when she walked past.

Nanna was so ashamed at being the talk of the town that she lost her mind a little. She developed dementia which developed at an unusually rapid rate. Within a year she was in a nursing home. Between you and me, I think she didn't have actual dementia at all. I think, like Mum used to say about Grandad, that Nanna had a mental breakdown from the shame of it all.

Nanna was dead in less than two years.

Mum and Dad went to the funeral, but Pauline and I didn't. Val and Sheila didn't go either.

You'll be pleased to hear that Grandad never did get his plaque put up in the church. No trees were planted in his name.

There is one person I do feel sorry for, and that is my dad. He really did love his father and spent his whole life trying to make him proud. It must be so confusing for him to now be ashamed of the man he spent his whole life trying to impress. And it must have been awful to know what his own dad had done to his sisters and daughter. And I sincerely believe he knew nothing of what was happening to his sisters while growing up. Everything about the way he has reacted tells me that is true. Plus, he was so much younger than his sisters. Grandad had probably stopped the abuse by the time Dad would have been old enough to notice.

I was so afraid that this revelation would ruin my relationship with Dad. I thought he would be angry with me, or somehow blame me without wanting to. I thought he would hate me a little bit for accusing his beloved father of something so terrible. I even thought he might be disgusted with me, that I was somehow soiled goods, or polluted in some way.

But he doesn't resent me at all. Our relationship did change, but if anything, it changed for the better. Dad seemed to draw me closer after the revelations came out. As the years went on, I came to think this was a kind of apology. He was a typical, burly man who didn't show his feelings easily. He never did come out and say, 'I'm sorry, I should have protected you better, it's my fault'. But something told me that's actually what he was thinking. I thought he would blame me. But really, I think he blamed himself.

I knew I couldn't spend my life eaten up in hate and resentment. I knew I needed to get on with life. If not, somehow it felt like he would win. So since I have become older, overcome my bulimia and had my own family, I have resolved to have the best life possible. I often hear on television that abusers were usually abused themselves, and that abused people usually go on to abuse their own children. When I hear that, it makes me so angry I could kick the television, because I was abused and I would never harm a hair on my babies' heads. I would never stand by if I knew I could stop a child being hurt. If someone threatened my children, I would commit murder to protect them.

I try to find reasons to be grateful for my life, because I know that is a good way to let go of the past. So here's something good that came out of all this horror: my experiences with the Evil Grandad from Hell have left me with one ambition – to be the best mum I possibly can. My children are the light of my life, and I do everything in my power to keep them safe and happy.

And when my children have children, I will be the best nanna a child has ever had.

If you enjoyed this book, please check out

Ugly Child

Another shocking childhood memoir
by Kate Skylark as *Siobhan Lennon*

It's finally time for Kate to tell her own story. *Ugly Child* is the touching and shocking account of the author's own childhood bullying and sexual abuse hell. Kate's real name is Siobhan. This is her horrendous story…

Life was never easy for little Siobhan. Born with cerebral palsy, she already had extra difficulties to contend with. But her disability isn't her only problem. For Siobhan, life is a nightmare of constant verbal and physical attacks. The abuse soon turns more serious, even violent. And Siobhan plunges deeper into a relentless hell of daily attacks.

As the abuse escalates, Siobhan begins to fear for her life. The story builds to a powerful crescendo, and one final, shocking act of sexual violence changes the lives of all concerned for ever.

No child should have to undergo such torment.
For every book sold,
a donation will be made to the NSPCC.

Printed in Great Britain
by Amazon